EDDIE THOMPSON

# POETRY
*Decaffed*

~~~

*More verses about life*

with drawings by Peter Osborne

EDDIE THOMPSON

# POETRY
## *Decaffed*

~~~

*More verses about life*

with drawings by Peter Osborne

**MEREO**
Cirencester

## Mereo Books

1A The Wool Market Dyer Street Cirencester Gloucestershire GL7 2PR

An imprint of Memoirs Publishing www.mereobooks.com

Poetry Decaffed: 978-1-86151-797-5

First published in Great Britain in 2016
by Mereo Books, an imprint of Memoirs Publishing

Copyright ©2017

Eddie Thompson has asserted his Right under the Copyright Designs and Patents Act 1988 to be identified as the author of this work.

This book is a work of fiction and except in the case of historical fact any resemblance to actual persons living or dead is purely coincidental.

A CIP catalogue record for this book is available from the British Library.

This book is sold subject to the condition that it shall not by way of trade or otherwise be lent, resold, hired out or otherwise circulated without the publisher's prior consent in any form of binding or cover, other than that in which it is published and without a similar condition, including this condition being imposed on the subsequent purchaser.

The address for Memoirs Publishing Group Limited can be found at
www.memoirspublishing.com

The Memoirs Publishing Group Ltd Reg. No. 7834348

The Memoirs Publishing Group supports both The Forest Stewardship Council® (FSC®) and the PEFC® leading international forest-certification organisations. Our books carrying both the FSC label and the PEFC® and are printed on FSC®-certified paper. FSC® is the only forest-certification scheme supported by the leading environmental organisations including Greenpeace. Our paper procurement policy can be found at
www.memoirspublishing.com/environment

Cover design and artwork - Ray Lipscombe

Typeset in 9/15pt Bembo
by Wiltshire Associates Publisher Services Ltd. Printed and bound in Great Britain by Printondemand-Worldwide, Peterborough PE2 6XD

# CONTENTS

Short ones

Limericks

Six-liners

Long ones

Longer ones

# INTRODUCTION

A few of these verses are autobiographical,
Some are reasonable, but most are just plain laughable
Yet when all is said and done, they are therapeutical,
Better indeed than many a pharmaceutical.
This is all very well, but I can't help feeling,
That some – how shall I say – are a touch too revealing.

# ABOUT THE AUTHOR

Eddie Thompson is an expatriate Manxman who settled in Milton Keynes with Enid, his Welsh wife, and daughters Kirsty and Gill in 1981 (so not quite pioneers) after serving twenty-six years in the army.

After confidence boosting three-minute appearances in open mike sessions in 'Tongue in Chic' performances in Wolverton, hosted by Mark Niel, Milton Keynes' Poet Laureate, he decided to put his verses into print. He continues to quarry a rich seam.

He thanks Peter Osborne for giving his time and talent to marry up his delightful artwork to the poems.

# DEDICATION

To Rosie and Noel Parsons

Also by Eddie Thompson

Poetry Lite
Poetry Free Range

# SHORT ONES

## Writing Rhymes

If you're looking for praise - you're not going to get it
If you're hoping they'll sell - best forget it
If you throw them away - you're bound to regret it
If it wants to be part of your life - then let it.

# SHORT ONES

## Contents

Autumn Leaves

Camomile Tea

Revelation from Above

"A Little Something in your Drink, Sir?"

Conniburrow Pond (4)

Flying High

Malthus, where are you now?

Thought for Today

Mysterious Measures

Voices

Putting one's foot in it

Conniburrow Pond (5)

Unorthodoxy

A Mantra

Failures

Hilary O'Donoghue

Philosophy

Dot Com Rage

It's May

## AUTUMN LEAVES

The falling leaves lie ankle deep,
The seasons' cycle turns and nature falls asleep,
Reds, yellows and ambers, in the autumn sun they glitter,
And still they have a role to play, they cover up the litter.


## CAMOMILE TEA

Camomile tea has a calming effect,
It's relaxing, restful and provides time to reflect
But take care; it's perfectly possible to overdose
And to enter a state known as 'camomile comatose'.


## REVELATION FROM ABOVE

Our friends had a mirror on their bathroom ceiling,
I pondered on its use, and found it quite appealing
My daydreams ran riot, but I left the room appalled,
For 'twas there I discovered that I was going bald.


## "A LITTLE SOMETHING IN YOUR DRINK, SIR?"

The effects of ageing are becoming clear,
And are far too many to mention here,
But there's one that I find deeply distressing,
It's undeniably distinctly depressing —
Drops from my nose fall into my beer.

## CONNIBURROW POND (4)

They meet at the pond, to chew their khat,
Though the leaf is illegal, it isn't that
Their lives can't be fun, that's not hard to believe,
It's the gross amount of litter they leave.


## FLYING HIGH

"I wandered lonely as a cloud,
That floats on high o'er vales and hills";[1]
Floating high above the crowds!
Had he swallowed Coleridge's pills?


## MALTHUS, WHERE ARE YOU NOW?

Between us and other species, there is a sharp distinction
Our population dominates, daily expanding,
Earth's finite resources, greedily demanding,
Causing other species to face imminent extinction.


## THOUGHT FOR TODAY

Your thought for today, as you lie in bed this morning,
Glancing through the curtains, an icy cold day dawning,
Is to think that surely it cannot be a sin,
To luxuriate in bed, with a lovely long lie in.

---

The opening lines of William Wordsworth's poem 'I wandered lonely as a cloud', also known as 'Daffodils'.

# MYSTERIOUS MEASURES

Megabytes, Megahertz and Milibands

# VOICES

It's not so much what you say
But the voice that you use with which to say it
That gives your personality away.

# PUTTING ONE'S FOOT IN IT

Head up, chest out, pull your shoulders back,
That's the way to deflect the flak
Right, then how to avoid stepping in the trap,
Of that smelly, ubiquitous, canine crap?

# CONNIBURROW POND (5)

Conniburrow Pond for foreigners has become a social hub,
Expats gather to drink and chat beneath ash and ancient oak,
And in the midst of this Tower of Babel, lies the core of a classical joke,
An Azerbaijani, a Hungarian and a Manxman walked into a pub…

# UNORTHODOXY

Most of us warm to the unorthodox,
But I draw the line at men wearing frocks,
And yes, I know, I shouldn't deride it,
As they say, "Don't knock it 'till you've tried it."

# EDDIE THOMPSON

## A MANTRA

"Something nice will happen today."
It's as good a mantra as any,
And if events depend upon what we say,
My positive perks will be many.

## FAILURES

Yes, there have been a few failures along the way,
That I would never deny,
But those who have never failed, they say,
Have really failed to try.

## HILARY O'DONOGHUE

I challenge any one of you,
To sit unmoved upon a pew,
Whilst listening to her lovely voice.
What's her name? You wanna clue?
It's Hilary O'Donoghue.

## PHILOSOPHY

Defined as 'the pursuit of wisdom' — what a bloomin' farce,
In the words of the sage Jim Royle, 'Philosophy my arse'.

## DOT COM RAGE

If I had a 9 mil Browning shooter,
I'd empty it into this cussed computer.

## IT'S MAY

"It's May, it's May, the lusty month of May,"
You know what this means men, you know what they say,
"Stiffen the sinews", your intentions harden,
Get out the back and sort out the garden.

# LIMERICKS

Some like their poetry clinical,
To all other forms they are cynical
At verses like this
They will boo and hiss,
But the limerick, to me, is the pinnacle.

# LIMERICKS

CONTENTS

Going Going…
The Poetry Reading
What's in a Name
Me Melismas
Four More Limericks
Gabriel Rossetti
Duty Bound
Decolletage

## GOING GOING...

It's no use me railing and wailing,
Let's face it, my memory is failing,
Maybe its 'free space' is decreasing,
Or maybe its cogs need regreasing.
Whatever the cause, my life it's derailing.

## THE POETRY READING

A poetry reading, that might be tough
It's something not played off the cuff
Without any doubt
Rude ones are out
So I ask myself, will I have enough 'stuff'?

## WHAT'S IN A NAME?

There was a fine lady from Leicester,
Whose only son was a jester
A possible cause
Was their odd surname, Draws,
For the name she had given him was Chester.

## ME MELISMAS

Me melismas are giving me jip,
They've spread from me leg to me hip,
To put it politely
They're somewhat unsightly,
What's more, they're disturbing me kip.

## FOUR MORE LIMERICKS

Yes, our memories are fraying,
And we're gradually greying,
And I hasten to venture
Don't mention dementia,
What was I saying?

For sheer delight, a whispered word,
But then again, you may have heard,
By the Bishop's crozier
I swear it's ambrosia,
It's Rita's home-made lemon curd.

What! try positive thinking,
Have you been drinking?
Away and bake
Your sunshine cake,
This vessel isn't sinking.

If you've something to say, say it in rhyme,
If you lose the rhythm, that isn't a crime,
But by St Peter
Avoid strict metre,
It distorts your message every time.

## GABRIEL ROSSETTI

Gabriel Rossetti, we're led to believe,
Was a talented tup, prone to deceive,
With a Hey Diddle-Diddle,
He exhumed Lizzie Siddal
With sorrow subdued, his poems to retrieve.

## DUTY BOUND

For men it is an undoubted duty
To inform a rare and forward beauty
That her countenance divine
Resembles fine wine,
Full-bodied, fragrant and fruity.

## DÉCOLLETAGE

It is blatantly glaring that women are wearing
A décolletage increasingly daring.
This behoves a man
As best as he can
To avert his gaze from what they are baring.

# SIX-LINERS

I've just discovered, oh pity of pities,
These aren't really poems, they are merely ditties,
But all along I've been realistic,
Some might say pessimistic,
Aware of the cynics and poetry definers,
I've referred to them always as 'silly six-liners'.

# SIX-LINERS

## CONTENTS

Recruiting
Re a New National Anthem
Mons Pubis: where exactly is it?
Rosella
Bliss
Bliss (2)
My ABC of Poets
Mike O'Connor
Facial Gardening
Allure
Fun
Edward's Psychedelic Socks
Losing Interest
Christmas
Chaos?
Speech as Song
My Ear-Worm
Pat Powell
The Five Bra Find
The Elixir of Life
Phased Out?
Our Geography Tutor
Placebos
The Oral Tradition
Hacking at a Hacker
Enid's Cutting her Toe-nails
Have I got this right?

The Front Row
A "Kebab" Poem
Full Circle?
Diary Keepers
Music Theory
Prayer
The Road to Annalong
Appeasement
The Silent 'H'
It's Tai Chi for Me
Beware the Demagogues
The Conversion
The Duality of One
What's in a Name? (2)
Dylan Thomas
My Favourite Vitamin
One Last Time
Plato and Poetry
Retirement
SWs with Attitude and Form
Ease Together
Trying, in every sense
Tanks for the Memory
Vowels
December 2008
I Have a Hernia O

# RECRUITING

Four little litter pickers, picking in a row,
Oliver and Emily, Madeleine and Joe,
Four little locusts, to pick the area clean,
Hoovering up the litter, keeping MK green,
Four little leading lights, recycling bags in hand,
Come and swell the ranks of this lovely little band.

Sept '11
*(For a visit by environmentalists and NAG members to Southwood School, Conniburrow, Milton Keynes.)*


# RE A NEW NATIONAL ANTHEM

It's time for a new national anthem, say some,
Something befitting the flag and the drum,
Something to stir the gathered throng,
Something to carry the crowd along,
Something close to the military marches,
What about that tune from 'The Archers'?[2]


# MONS PUBIS, WHERE EXACTLY IS IT?

Mons Pubis? Ah yes, I'm pretty sure it's south of the Severn,
It's a chocolate-box village, somewhere in Devon.
No no, you're too far west,
It's a village in Hampshire, on the banks of the Test.
You're both wrong, check it out on the map,
It's off the M1, in the Watford Gap.

---

[2] Once suggested, on stage, by comedian Billy Connolly.

## ROSELLA

Perhaps we should tell the RSPB
That a parrot is perched in our pear tree
A parrot in MK! Truly incredible,
A cascade of colour, a picture indelible
It rules the roost in its red balaclava,
And amongst the magpies, it has caused a palaver.

## BLISS

Euphoria I can live without,
And "Joys excelling", what's that about?
No; my blissful experience is, in the main,
Startlingly simple and to many, mundane,
For me the ultimate pleasure is knowing
That my headache, at last, is definitely going.

## BLISS (2)

There's a spring in my step,
A new-found pep,
I'm invigorated,
Rejuvenated,
What joy, what men,
'Poms' Twelve, Aussies Ten.

## MY ABC OF POETS

Her poetry diverts us from our fears and cares,
With her West Country burr, the lovely Pam Ayres,
To many he is their poet of choice,
That lyrical Welshman, humorous Max Boyce,
Her poetry scans such depth and scope,
The wonderfully witty Wendy Cope.

## MIKE O'CONNOR

Mike is dying, he knows the score,
He's been given six months, we're hoping for more
His approach to this is amazingly Stoic,
It's more than that, it's downright heroic.
Mike and Rita are examples to us all,
And when my turn comes, on their courage I will call.   May '11

## FACIAL GARDENING

Why does it grow there — this nasal hair?
How does it flourish without lawn feed or care?
It's long strong and straight, like unwanted weeds
Should I curl them, unfurl them, or market the seeds?
Then there's the foliage that sprouts from my ears,
That Enid will trim — with the garden shears.

## ALLURE

This word 'allure',
It's French to be sure
And to 'lure' it must be related
You know, when the hook has been baited
In such a way as to lure us cunningly into a trap,
Where often, if not always, we end up in the crap.

## FUN

Fun and frolics no longer figure, the trail has long gone cold
They've gone, along with vim and vigour, the price of growing old
When I think of the fun we had, years ago when young,
It's like a violin well played, like a song well sung,
So, reinstate the 'Minster of Fun', David What'shisname,
Let 'Fun for All' be the cry, 'Fun for All' the aim.

## EDWARD'S PSYCHEDELIC SOCKS

Glamorous women with their golden locks,
Ladies in their floral frocks,
All lovely to behold
But I can see, on a centre-fold,
A sight that would generate shocks,
Edward, wearing only his psychedelic socks.

## LOSING INTEREST

Losing interest is an Amber Alert,
The first step towards becoming inert,
Losing interest in all our activities,
Sees us becoming moribund antiquities,
For once we enter the interest-free zone,
We're on Red Alert and depression prone.

## CHRISTMAS

Christmas? I'd like to make it perfectly clear,
(For reasons I refuse to discuss with you here)
That I'm with Oliver Cromwell on this,
It should be banned, go ahead, boo and hiss,
OK, just one, haven't you heard the shopkeepers singing?
"Praise the Lord and keep the tills ringing".

## CHAOS?

It's something that I've always suspected,
Everything is interconnected
In random choice I can't believe,
Life, as I see it, is an intricate weave
Of mysterious guide lines, like Zen navigation,
That nudge us towards our life's destination.

*(With a nod to the late Douglas Adams and his character Dirk Gently.)*

## SPEECH AS SONG

Some phrases more than others have a certain swing,
Some phrases, moreover, encourage us to sing
Take as an example, 'Me old brass jam pan',
(Which begs to rhyme with 'A Chinese sampan),
It's the rhythm, the stresses, the ups and the downs,
It's akin to singing; well, that's how it sounds.


## MY EAR-WORM

I have an ear-worm,
There's no need to raise medical alarms,
It's not the worm that makes you squirm,
It's the musical worm that charms and calms
It's as if I've caught a benevolent germ,
It's Bernstein's beautiful Chichester Psalms.


## PAT POWELL

Pat,
Our life enhancing, effervescent, old friend, Pat,
Is ill,
Seriously ill,
And of course, there is no fast track back
All we ask is that we get Pat back.                    Nov'12

## THE FIVE BRA FIND

It was the weirdest find for quite a while,
Five bras together, by the pond, in a pile
Had a fetishist, by his conscience been pricked?
And off-loaded his haul, all of them nicked,
After a somewhat perfunctory trawl
I figured, for my wife, they'd be far too small.

## THE ELIXIR OF LIFE

It's the elixir of life, it makes us shine,
It clears our veins and makes us frisky,
It lessens strife and makes us feel fine,
Absorb all you can, it just isn't risky,
This nectar's revealed in the following line,
I'm referring of course, to Sanatogen Wine.

# PHASED OUT?

I'm looking to start a new phase in my life,
One I can share with Enid, my wife,
The front runner right now is cooking,
On second thoughts I'll continue looking,
But I have a feeling that just may be true,
It's pointless looking, as phases find you.


# OUR GEOGRAPHY TUTOR

Our geography tutor leant to the left,
At the fall of the wall she was left bereft,
An ardent apologist of the USSR
She kept back-copies of the *Morning Star*[3].
Later she relied on Ginkgo Biloba,
And was known to her students as Pinko Pulova.


# PLACEBOS

"Take these pills, they'll ease your pain",
It's the doctor's authority conning your brain
Though there's no active drug in the pills,
They sometimes ease imaginary ills
So what if we're conned if it eases our plight?
Should we view religion in a similar light?

---

[3] The only socialist daily newspaper in the English-speaking world.

# THE ORAL TRADITION

Enid, my wife, is totally exasperated
By tales that she reckons are grossly exaggerated
But what Enid doesn't realize
Is that these 'tall tales' are far from lies,
They're story-telling in the old tradition,
Where truth hinders not the spoken rendition.


# HACKING AT A HACKER

Yes, for sure, I could cheerfully neuter,
He who recently hacked my computer,
The punishment I'd inflict may not fit the crime,
It's total immersion in a pit of lime
No, too much, but to ease my frustration,
I will settle instead for a crude castration.            Aug '16


# ENID'S CUTTING HER TOE-NAILS

Enid's cutting her toe-nails, take heed, you have been told
Please don't enter the room, I beg you, don't be so bold,
From twelve feet her clippings can kill,
Ignore me at your peril, I assure you they will,
They fly like shrapnel around the room,
If you enter without a tin hat, prepare to meet your doom.

## HAVE I GOT THIS RIGHT?

I tuned into Radio 4 Long Wave yesterday,
And heard an excited commentator say,
"…it's in the air and they're shouting CAT SHIT!"
Well, surely, it's not beyond the wit,
Of the cricketing authorities by now to have found,
A means of keeping cats out of the ground.

## THE FRONT ROW

Singing on the front row the dread in me explodes,
Wrong rhythm notes and words, totally exposed.
If I'm singing there again next week,
Without a paddle, up the creek,
Then it's time to face the sobering fact,
It's time to leave, before I'm sacked.

## A "KEBAB POEM"[4]

A kebab poem like this has a skewer running right down its middle,
Purists may see it as an impure form of poetry,
Many will shout 'Horse manure' and suchlike insults,
And call them weak and poor, insecure, namby-pamby flim-flam
But hopefully some, fewer I know, will smile at the style.
Personally I like its lure; it's different, that's for sure.

---

[4] Kebab Poems; mentioned on BBC Radio 4 'Front Row' 19.2.09.

# FULL CIRCLE?

Full circle our society has turned,
As religion it has openly spurned
It's atheists who now strut and tut,
The shoe is on the other foot,
This disbelief carries risk and danger,
So I'm hedging my bets with Pascal's Wager.

# DIARY KEEPERS

Yes, it's undeniable,
Diaries make interesting reading,
And they're fairly reliable
Records of the lives that we are leading
But I hold the view, fairly viable,
That the writers for readers are pleading

# MUSIC THEORY

It's a pain in the proverbial, this music theory stuff,
All I want to do is sing, but that is not enough,
First-inversion triads and scales diatonic
Why do I have to know these, these scales diabolic?
So I'll say it again — and yes, I'm in a huff,
All I want to do is sing, not write the bloomin' stuff.

# PRAYER

How do prayers work? It's a mystery I'm looking at anew,
And yes, of course you're right; my question implies that they do,
Some say there are guardian angels, awaiting a personal call,
They're our personal in-house helper, available to all
My experience suggests that something like this may be true,
It works, that's all we need to know, not how, or why, or who.

# THE ROAD TO ANNALONG

'What means this anxious waiting throng',
Along the road to Annalong?
Wenches washing windscreens,
All with nothing on,
They think they've found their Avalon,
Along the road to Annalong.

# APPEASEMENT

Political Correctness decrees
That "Christian" names are out,
From now on, if you please,
(And this must surely hurt the devout),
"First" names is the word we should use.
Political Correctness is turning the screws.

## THE SILENT 'H'

Honestly, on my honour,
The 'H' you do not sing,
It's Osanna! Osanna!
Give the word an authentic ring
By giving the 'H' the verbal axe,
Think 'orrible 'enry, from 'alifax.


## IT'S TAI CHI FOR ME

It's Tai Chi for me,
It's the nearest I dare get to old-time PT,
It's slow and it's gentle and it's good for the circulation,
It's good for our inner organs, and even constipation
It's best done in the morning, with other early risers,
If only I could master the warm-up exercises.


## BEWARE THE DEMAGOGUES

Follow them and you'll find yourself in a metaphorical fog,
I speak of the deadly dangerous charismatic demagogue
Shun their beguiling rhetoric, and the emotional appeal,
For to follow him or her is to make with the devil a deal.
The unmistakable feature of practising demagogues
Is their unshakable belief that they are indeed demi-gods.

# THE CONVERSION

To non-conformism I can't conform,
To organized religion I cannot warm
Away with things Episcopalian,
I want rites and rituals Bacchanalian.
So what, if you think I'm Brahms and Liszt
You see before you a Hedonist.

# THE DUALITY OF ONE

The personal pronouns 'you' and 'I'
Have by the hoity-toity and those on high
Been replaced by 'one', and one wonders why.

Is her highness told, when to bed they've gone,
Before any sex is embarked upon,
That 'One would like to give one one'?[5]

# WHAT'S IN A NAME? (2)

Being called by your Christian name, to me that's all about
A kind of verbal touching, a sort of reaching out,
It's a warm attempt to enter
Your guarded garden centre
So names, they are important, do you get the gist?
They are a confirmation that we really do exist.

---

[5] A phrase used by comedian Billy Connelly

## DYLAN THOMAS

Dylan Thomas, teller of tall tales,
Welsh, but sometimes unkind to Wales,
With words a wizard, and a difficult man to host,
Being utterly dependent, he would charm money from most.
If his personal behaviour was seen as heinous,
His poetry was that of a genius.


## MY FAVOURITE VITAMIN

Some may say you're being idle,
Sitting in the sun
But you're ensuring your survival,
And the treatment's fun.
More than that, the treatment's free,
So please, all praise, for Vitamin D.


## ONE LAST TIME

Lying on my death bed, with Enid sitting near,
I'd beckon Enid closer, so that she could hear
My weak and whispered parting, my ultimate 'good night'
Before the final fatal dimming of the light,
And I'd whisper in her ear, through a frail enfeebled cough,
Thanks for all you've done En dear, and TURN THE BLOODY TAPS OFF!

# PLATO AND POETRY[6]

Plato objected to poetry because he thought
The poet to be a disreputable sort
As they never meant what they said.
Poets, to Plato, lacked a certain street cred!
What Plato thought of poets we have now been made aware;
What poets thought of Plato has yet to be laid bare.


# RETIREMENT

Now well into retirement,
Sort of surplus to requirement
I find that writing silly verses,
Helps to fend off ageing's curses
That, and a caring, lovely wife,
Steers me clear of mental strife.


# SWS WITH ATTITUDE AND FORM

Swank swagger swell,
Swot sweat swirl,
Swig swear swipe,
Swine swill swamp,
Swish swede swinging
Swizz swag swindle.

---

[6] Letters to the Editor TLS June 10th 2016. RMJ Dammann, Poynings Brighton

## EASE TOGETHER

We're known to some as E and E,
Which sounds like a hospital ward,
And we sign ourselves as Ed 'n' En,
Which sounds like somewhere abroad,
But it matters not which or whether,
Just so long as we're together.


## TRYING, IN EVERY SENSE

Alas, alas, woe is me,
I cannot write good poet-tree,
But then again, what does it matter?
It is to most but idle chatter.
But they are wrong and I will write,
Even though it turns out trite.


## TANKS FOR THE MEMORY

When will I have a restful dream
Of water over stones, in a fast-flowing stream?
Or walking the dog over hills and heather,
On the Isle of Man, in gorgeous spring weather?
Or singing the 'Messiah' in a mixed voice choir?
Instead of tank commanders shouting "SABOT DOT 2 FIRE".

## VOWELS

A toast to that gallant little group of five,
Our vowels; may they and their diphthongs continue to thrive
Without them, where and what would our language be?
A series of grunts in a cave or a tree?
In English there are five, and Welsh has seven,
But Welsh is the language spoken in heaven.


## DECEMBER 2008

It's early December, damp, dark and dismal,
It's worse than that, it's bloody abysmal
But grit the teeth lads, it's going to get worse,
The 'good times' have slipped into bloody reverse.
The recession and Christmas are coming together,
That's got to be worse than the bloody weather.

# I HAVE A HERNIA O

Hey Ho,

I've a hernia O,

Thus goeth an old Tudor sing-along,

With a hey nonny no,

I singeth in woe,

For my hernia much worry doth bring along.

# LONG ONES

These verses lack purpose
Between me and you, that's not strictly true
I'll understand if you say they're bland,
Yet one or two state a serious view
And some, as they say, are a little risqué,
But they're far from taxing, in fact they're relaxing
And they put a few coppers in the choir's coffers.

# LONG ONES

## CONTENTS

Rita O'Connor
Standard 5a 1946
Choice
Shamanism Revisited
Four Quatrains
A Walk in the Wood
The Magic of Cinema
The Quaver
Harmony
The Chair
Doodling with Doggerel
The Wine List
Existentialism
Dramatic Events
Just Talking
A Dilemma
Culture
Edward's Obituary
Guardian Angels
The Draw
It's Not Cricket
My Computer
Conniburrow Boulevard
Iambic Pentameter
Life's only Guarantee
Conniburrow Pond (2)
Louise Wilcox
Maureen Burrows (1945-2008)
It'll Come Back To Me
July 2013

"O Fortuna", The Wheel of Fortune
A Toast
The Angel in the Wallpaper
Indelible
A Broken Society?
Handel's Dixit Dominus (2)
Please, Not a Word
Retirement (2)
Lady Jane Grey- an Apology
Bruckner's Mass in E Minor
Bedsocks and Broomsticks
Well there we are then- it's official
A Windsock, Anyone?
One for the Committee
Hyperbole
Liz, Demi-Johns and LSDs
The Trunk
Mark Niel
Place (2)
Inner-city Farming
Our Souls
Recruiting for the Chorale
Body Parts as Metaphor
The Festive Season
Voice Procedure
Give me an L
Dear Tom
Post Audition Blues

## RITA O'CONNOR

I want to honour
Rita O'Connor,
To sing her praises
In suitable, serious, eloquent phrases
But I can't, Rita wasn't that sort,
If I started, she'd very soon cut me short.
So what can I say?
It will have to be brief, she would want it that way.
So I want her soul to be bathed in white,
It's what she deserves after shedding her light
On all she knew,
Rita; pure, kind and true,
How privileged we are to have met you,
We will never, ever, forget you.    June '13

## STANDARD 5A 1946

Look! My nineteen-forty-six school reports,
Complete with cutting comments that I see as ugly warts,
My English work is marked "Disgraceful",
To my parents that must have been at least distasteful.
In the Intelligence Test I fared even worse,
"Dreadful" is the comment, concise and terse
In the General Report I am "Disappointing".
What is that but with shame anointing?
And yet, about them I feel strangely proud,
Although at the time I must have been cowed –
Sitting in the thicko's place

Gazing, dreaming, lost in space,
My star chart held neither silver nor gold,
For all this, there were reasons that time would unfold
But reports like this, on a lad just ten years,
Would cut far too deep, cuts that bled tears
It took some time, and though I turned it around,
The tenor of these reports never fails to astound.

# CHOICE

Almost as a mantra, the Tories will push choice,
Choice, choice and choice again, in a loud persistent voice
But we know deep down that with choice there is a hitch,
(Even amongst those who can afford to choose – the affluent, the rich),
It's the anxiety inherent in the choosing,
"If I make the wrong choice, what would we be losing?"
Should the choice be misguided, someone will have to atone
So maybe choice we would do without, if the truth be known.

That's what the existentialists say, and they could be right
The theory may explain why some of us are so uptight.
It's an interesting philosophy, and I hear what they say,
But all of us face choices, and we face them every day.

# SHAMANISM REVISITED

My grandmother read tea-leaves and had a cure for warts,
This memory returns me to half-remembered Shamanic thoughts
Shamans are problem solvers and primitive prototype priests
Who find solutions in nature, aided by the spirits of birds and beasts
They also act as doctors, whose primary concern is the soul,
And in primitive (early) societies, they are seen as a social control,
With the rhythmic beat of the drum, they enter a trance-like state,
And with the audience enthralled, they pass through their spiritual gate
They journey into the spirit world, dressed in skins, furs or feathers,
From eagles, bears, possibly hares, or maybe buffalo leathers
Their skill is always hereditary, often missing a generation,
And is honed by years of training, which includes a near-death sensation.
Please don't think they're confined to Siberia,
The Inuit, the Amazon, or Liberia
For I've seen one working here in MK,
It's an interesting phenomenon, that's what I want to say.


# FOUR QUATRAINS

This little refrain,
A simple quatrain,
Is short and sweet,
Concise, complete.


Quatrains can be either
Good or bad or neither,
Their one big pull?
They're too short to be dull.

Yet another appeal,
Which to most is ideal,
The quatrain's four lines
Focuses minds.

This fourth quatrain
Is taxing my brain
It shouldn't, I know,
But it does – does it show?

# A WALK IN THE WOOD

A car battery, a microwave oven, beer cans
Cigarette packets, lighters, sandwich wrappings, beer cans
Crisp packets, a burnt-out motor-bike, beer cans
An old bike, plastic bottles, glass bottles, beer cans
Small plastic bags of dog crap hanging on bushes, beer cans
A garden fence post, the base encased in concrete, beer cans
An umbrella and foot pump (both broken), beer cans
Undelivered newspapers, a porno mag, an office chair, beer cans
Two vandalized trees, a dead cat in a cardboard box, beer cans
A lamp-post garlanded with a bicycle tyre, beer cans
A shopping trolley, an ironing board, plastic bags, beer cans
Beer cans.

# THE MAGIC OF CINEMA

Tonight we're off to the 'pictures',
Leaving at home reality
We're escaping life and its strictures,
To turn our backs on normality.

We're going to be launched into outer space,
With popcorn, Coke and comfy seats,
We'll relocate the human race
And suck during lift-off boiled sweets.

Cinema takes us by the hand,
Plies us with laughter and tears,
It leads us into fantasy land
To forget our worries and fears.

Isn't that what cinema is for,
To play with our emotions?
To speak, at length, to our inner core,
Across desert sands and oceans?

Look at cinemas' names
Al Hambra, Odeon, Palace
Each one offering exotic claims
That take us from Durham to Dallas.

Ecstasy, that's what cinema's about,
Stepping out of ourselves
To escape a life of debt and doubt,
Whilst deeper and deeper the story delves.

## THE QUAVER

A quaver,
The whole quaver — to hold and savour.

The semi-quaver,
Half the whole but retaining its flavour.

The demi-semi quaver,
Small and perfectly formed — a right little raver.

The hemi-demi, semi-quaver,
The blink of an eye — the infinitesimal time-saver.

## HARMONY

To be in harmony with others, that's what singing's about
To lift your voice in song is akin to the primeval shout
It's a pressure release valve, relieving stress,
It's therapeutic, a mental caress
"Harmony, an agreement of feeling…"
Of its definitions, that's the most appealing
That it's all about feelings, in my mind there's no doubt,
To be in harmony with others, that's what singing's about.

# THE CHAIR

Visiting our friends in Chesham recently,
We entered an antique shop and there
Enid spotted an ageing, wicker chair
That seemed to be pleading, like a dog in a rescue centre,
Try me, buy me,
So we did.

What intrigues me is its history,
Which, of course, must remain a mystery.

I can see it in a hotel sun-lounge
In between the wars,
Its occupant sporting plucked eyebrows and a cigarette holder
Through which she smokes 'Craven 'A' for her throat's sake',
Witnessing a gay young blade breezing in through the French windows
Asking, 'Anyone for tennis?'
Unaware that his short life will soon be snuffed out
In the coming second worldwide conflagration.

Or again, I see it on the deck of an ocean-going liner,
Sailing to, or from, India, or Burma, or Malaya
Supporting the bottom of a Colonial administrator, or his wife, (POSH of course),
Drinking copious quantities of quality gin
Laced with primaquine, or was it nivaquine?
Or maybe chloroquine or Paludrine?
To keep at bay (they hoped) malaria.

It may be just a chair to you, but to me it has a presence,
And when I'm sitting in it I'm aware that it has supported
More illustrious bottoms than mine.
I hope that it won't be bored
In this new phase of its existence.

# DOODLING WITH DOGGEREL

A parallax corrector,

An income-tax collector,

A linen flax selector,

A candle-wax deflector,

A laid-back lax elector,

A roadside 'snax' inspector.

Yes, it's a time-wasting doodle,

But it has a musical lilt

And yes there are other things to do,

But I'm damned if I'll feel any guilt.

# THE WINE LIST

### *Rias Baixas Albarino*
"Fashionable and elegant with intense fruit, minerality and a long finish. Ideal with fish."
The promise: you won't be plying your date with pish.

### *Anjou Rouge AOP*
"Aromatic redfruits, herbaceous notes and hints of graphite. Perfect with cold meals."
Carries more than a hint of hemp and chewed pencil ends. Use to wash down jellied eels.

### *Fleurie*
"Scented and floral with fresh ripe cherries, redfruits and a touch of bramble spice."

*Bramble spice / Old Spice*
I'll have a Guinness please.

# EXISTENTIALISM

This could be the one for me, existentialism,
"To be or not to be?" and all that pessimism.

We're alone and adrift in a meaningless life,
A philosophy of freedom, doom, gloom and strife.

"I, Thou and It", with Buber and Nietzsche,
Where Sartre's a hit and Prozac's a feature.

We're in uncharted waters, without guiding light,
But something tells me this may not be right.

It preaches despair in unfathomable prose,
And tells us that life is a catalogue of woes.

But hang on a bit, this is getting depressing,
We're not in a pit; life can be a blessing.

I've given it some thought and I have now decided
That I'm pleased with my life and won't have it derided.

# DRAMATIC EVENTS

These Dramatic Events, they lie in wait, in hiding,
They have set for us an ambush, and their time they are biding
Your life is going well, you feel you're on a roll,
Then bang, they hit you, and you know you've no control
No one escapes them, something's keeping score,
It's life, it's fate, it's a universal law
What is important is how we react,
That determines how they change us, that's a universal fact.

## JUST TALKING

| | | |
|---|---|---|
| I blab | I bluster | I bellow |
| You gibber | You lecture | You vilify |
| He babbles | He argues | He rants |
| She twitters | She communicates | She addresses |
| We quibble | We spout | We whisper |
| You prattle | You waffle | You drone |
| They gabble | They gossip | They pontificate |

I am flannelling
You are flattering
He is ordering
She is chattering
We are nattering
You are twittering
They are wittering

## A DILEMMA

Someone's sleeping rough in a tent nearby,
Should this be reported, and if so, why?
He might be trying to hide,
Or maybe he's dead inside
I should offer our garage, as in the famous stable,
Invite him to our table,
Will I interfere?
Maybe not this year.


## CULTURE

Into our cultures we are all inculcated,
And if we are well-bred, we are then 'cultivated'.
This word 'cultivated' has several definitions,
Like bred artificially, in controlled conditions,
This entails breeding, ie inculcation, to instil,
A role for the family and society to fill
With mono, multi and sub there are cultures by the score,
It's a sociologist's dream, research for evermore
Whilst we may cherish our given, or chosen, cultures,
 Certain aspects provide fodder for vultures
Borders, language and religion can all be divisive,
Where the law of the jungle is often decisive
Along with cultural revolutions, cults and culture shock,
Beware sophisticated shepherds conning the gullible flock.

# EDWARD'S OBITUARY

Edward was an average bloke, well, probably just under,
School reports suggested his existence was a blunder.

Useless at football, and at cricket dropped his catches,
And throughout his army service, not a mention in dispatches.

Late in life he lamented his total lack of fame,
But being mediocre, he didn't have a claim.

He whispered in my ear as he was getting wearier,
"Tell me straight," he said," Have I really been inferior?"

"Seriously Edward," I said, choosing my words with some care,
"Had your life been an English essay, I'd be pleased to mark it "Fair".

Now facing his final assessment, standing there at the gate,
How nice if he heard; "Satisfactory, you're in, the rest will have to wait."


# GUARDIAN ANGELS

Guardian Angels, do they exist?
Some swear that they do
On this they insist,
Whilst we have to hope it's true.

But haven't you felt that calming presence,
Dispelling fear and fright?
(Surely, for angels, the core essence)
I have, which makes me think they might be right.

# THE DRAW

*(Capital One Cup, 2$^{nd}$ Round, 2014)*

MK Dons versus Manchester United,
What a draw! No wonder we're excited.
To win is improbable, a Herculean task,
But to play with the greats, what more could we ask?
Our giant-killing hopes the tie has ignited,
But whatever the result, with the draw we're delighted.

# THE SCORE

Tell me the score one more time,
Just tell me the score, let's forget the rhyme,
Tell it to me slowly; tell it to me loud,
Tell me the score; it makes me feel so proud,
Yes tell me the score so I can walk tall.
What a night, what a team, football heroes all.
MK DONS FOUR, MANCHESTER UNITED NIL.

# THERE'S MORE

First the draw, then the score
But wait, there's more
On Saturday, after winding down,
There's a tough league game with Crawley Town
Friend Bruce, from Nottingham, requested a ticket,
(A bowling coach, seeking a break from cricket)
And there at the kiosk a crew from the BBC,
To film the next customer, who happened to be me.
They were filming the knock-on effects of the game,
And gave me my fifteen seconds of fame.             Aug '14

## MY COMPUTER

"Buy a computer,
It'll change your life"
Said the IT recruiter.
"Roll on!" said the wife.

I bought one in June,
No change is in sight,
Like cheese on the moon,
It's one megabyte.


## IAMBIC PENTAMETER

Perimeter, parameter,
So what is a pentameter?
Well saints alive!
It's the measure of five.
Right, that I've got,
But five of what?
In this case iams.
Ah, tropical fruit.
No, not yams, iams,
It sounds like five scams,
So what's an iam?
It's an unstressed syllable, followed by one that is stressed
Of course, of course, silly me, I should have guessed,
Iambic pentameter is poetry speak,
It's a line with five iams, there is no mystique,
It's a rhythmic form of speech and part of poetic word-play.
That's it, no more, I'm off. Hip hip hooray!

# CONNIBURROW BOULEVARD

Conniburrow Boulevard

Is lined with London plane trees,

And grassy banks and verges,

It's half a mile long and perfectly straight,

And has a junior school at each end

There are several sheltered bus stops,

An Afro-Caribbean and European hair stylist,

Four crossroads, each with a grass-covered roundabout,

A small office for neighbourhood police,

Blocks of flats and HIMOs,

A large children's playground,

Two caffs, one of which is cyber,

A kebab stall and an off-licence,

Two corner shops and a tattoo and fetishwear parlour,

A Residents' Association Office,

One Rolls Royce,

A new and much-used Community Centre,

Litter-pickers in hi-vis vests,

A Halal meat shop,

Police in cars going about their business,

A sports field with a baseball diamond,

And a multi-cultural population.

In winter it looks weary, worn-out, battle scarred,

But in summer it is different, then it is CONNIBURROW BOULEVARD.

# LIFE'S ONLY GUARANTEE

Ah yes, life's ups and downs,
Its smiles and frowns,
This fairground ride, with its laughter and tears,
Its cheers and jeers,
Without which life would be dreary,
Totally weary
Remember life's only guarantee, things are going to change
And this roller-coaster ride our lives will rearrange.


# CONNIBURROW POND (2)

Conniburrow Pond as a tourist attraction?
Me? Unhinged? Well OK, maybe a fraction,
But we could dream up an 'ancient' story
About ducking witches, or other things equally gory;
Let's say it's a site of some Saxon skulduggery,
Or older still, some Roman thuggery
All taking place in this once 'hallowed' oasis.
Let's give it the aura of mysterious places,
Let's fish an artefact out of the pond,
Get an 'expert' to state it's a Druid's wand
Let's 'find' a page in an 'ancient' hand
That suggests the pond lies on sacred land
Let's put up the fancy info boards,
Let's go for various heritage awards.
It will never be a UNESCO site,
But let's pull together to improve its plight.

## LOUISE WILCOX

We want so much to please Louise
We want so much to seize Louise
And hug her 'till it hurts,
For she's eighty today,
Our cockney sparrow, our colourful jay
How lucky we are to know her,
How can we possibly show her
What a delight she is,
What a bright light she is?
To say 'Happy Birthday' doesn't come near
To what she means to all of us here.
So let's raise our glasses and let her know,
She's the best, the crest, the star of the show.                Nov '09


## MAUREEN BURROWS (1945-2008)

Dear Maureen,
How little we knew of you
(How little we know of anyone)
Passing quietly by, gentle, seemingly shy,
And yet you were:
A believer in Christ, thanks to Billy Graham,
A graduate in English Language and Literature,
A teacher of English and German,
A Lancashire lass come south,
A translator of documents in German for Bletchley Park Museum,
And much else besides.

But we knew none of this
Until your funeral service today at the Salvation Army Citadel
Here in Conniburrow.
How I want your faith to be rewarded.
You deserve your peace,
With your demons defeated.
Dear Maureen,
How little we knew of you.                                         Jan '09


# IT'LL COME BACK TO ME

Enid, Kirsty, Gillian and me,
Or should that be I?
So, Enid, Gill, Kirsty and I…
No, it doesn't roll off the tongue,
How about, Enid, Kirsty, Gill and myself?
Or, Enid, Gill, Kirsty and oneself?
No, too hoity-toity,
Then maybe, Enid, Kirsty, Gill and yours truly?
That's sort of OK,
But I'll stay with Enid, Kirsty, Gillian and me,
It feels right and it flows free,

Now that that is out of the way,
I've forgotten what I wanted to say.

# JULY 2013

What's the temperature today dear?
'Dunno, it's bloody hot.'
Are you going to paint the fence dear?
'No I'm bloody not.'
Then maybe cut the grass dear?
'Cut the bloody WHAT!'
What will the neighbours think dear?
'I don't give a bloody jot!'
The dog is due his walk dear,
'Thanks a bloody lot.'
You could do some ironing dear
'Have you lost the bloody plot?'
Well, will you make the tea then, dear?
'The milk is one big clot.'
Tommy next door does it, dear
'That's Tommy bloody rot!'
Could you fetch me a drink then dear?
'Are you on a bloody yacht?'
Why are you so LAZY dear?
'It's just so bloody hot.'

## "O FORTUNA", THE WHEEL OF FORTUNE

                                                    jubilation
                                 reputation
                                                          presentation
                            remuneration
                                                         adulation
                                liberation
                                                         obligation
                                reparation
                                                       tribulation
                             qualification
                                                 exasperation
                           revitalization
                                                     vexation
                           recreation
                                                  intoxication
                           relaxation
                                                  debilitation
                        affirmation
                                                   defamation
                        moderation
                                                 immoderation
                        restoration
                                                  realization
                       revocation
                                               consternation
                     reconciliation
                                               degradation
                       stabilization
                                               alienation
                        determination
                                                   isolation
                        reservation
                                               desperation
                         negotiation
                                             examination
                           recuperation
                                           humiliation
                               consultation   medication
                                       desolation

# A TOAST[7]

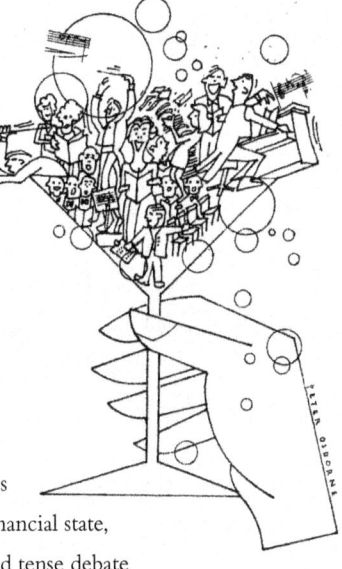

To Tim and Tom
And everyone
Who has previously conducted us
Or who formerly instructed us
To all our prior pianists,
To secretaries with membership lists,
To committees and chairs,
For their efforts and cares
To librarians, always under stress,
The degree of which we can only guess
To treasurers, those measurers of our financial state,
Whose audits always usher in a long and tense debate
To concert managers, what a task!
What a worry, what an ask,
To our sopranos, altos, tenors and basses,
(And the latters' lack of social graces)
To those who write the programmes, and decide on their design,
To those who sell the tickets, and to those who make mulled wine,

And before the celebration ends,
One more. To absent friends.                    March '13

---

[7] On the 40th anniversary of the Milton Keynes Chorale.

EDDIE THOMPSON

# THE ANGEL IN THE WALLPAPER

It was seventy years ago, give or take,
I was four, maybe five,
And ill
With whooping cough, or mumps, or measles, or chicken pox,
One of the many ailments that children got then,
So I was allowed to sleep in my parents' bed,
The 'big bed', in the front bedroom,
With the little fire lit, as a treat
(It was only lit when someone was ill).
I turned on my side to face the wall,
And there she was,
In the patterned wallpaper,
An angel.
Was it something in the medicine?
Was I hallucinating?
Was it childish imagination?
I lived in that house for a further twenty years, give or take,
And would often look for her again, in vain,
But I can still 'see' her, clearly,
In the wallpaper,
That angel.
Makes you think.

# INDELIBLE

Our memories apparently, cannot be erased
I find that quite incredible,
In truth I am amazed
That our pasts are undeniably indelible.

Flashbacks appear on our 'screens' without call
What brings them up we have no idea,
But whilst they are there, they do enthral,
Time is nothing and the image is clear.

As their name suggests, they have gone in a flash,
They can open old wounds but never bring closure,
They remain long enough to open a sash,
A window on our past exposure.

But Hey! These experiences made us what we are,
Be they good, bad, happy or sad
Cherish them, keep the door ajar,
Welcome them in, remember, and be glad.

# A BROKEN SOCIETY?

Massive cracks are appearing,
But it's not quite broken yet
Into the abyss we're peering,
Wondering how deep they will get
But steel ourselves we must,
And angrily break our silence
Over the death of trust,
And the rising tide of violence.

# PLEASE, NOT A WORD

Please keep it to yourself,
About my falling asleep in the public library
Maybe you're open to a little bribery?

I'll tell you what it was,
It's those new easy chairs in the reference section,
Apparently snores led to my detection.

It must have appeared
As if I was seeking shelter, in from the cold
Pretending to read, homeless and old.

There was one saving grace,
Well, in a way, more or less,
I had fallen asleep with the Times TLS.

# HANDEL'S DIXIT DOMINUS (2)

When composing this, was Handel high on 'stuff'?
And when I say high, I'm not talking snuff.
It screws me up completely,
So what if I'm talking indiscreetly?
It sends me home frustrated,
Depressed, down, weighted, deflated
To Dixit Dominus, I acknowledge defeat,
Not to do so, would be a deceit.


# RETIREMENT (2)

Of this 'keep busy' business I've really had enough,
The truth of it is — it's making me feel rough
I want to be bored,
Not worn out and floored,
I want to have time to defluff my navel,
To sit in the sun with a Worthy's Red Label
I want time to ponder on the purpose of life
To back a winning horse and then treat my wife.
I think, fair play, that I have done my whack,
And I want to feel the sun warm upon my back
Time to pity others at their daily grind,
And allow good music to unlock my mind.

## LADY JANE GREY — AN APOLOGY

An apology is due; and of course it's late in the day,
To the grievously wronged Lady Jane Grey.
We apologise and seek your forgiveness, dear Lady Jane,
For the cruel injustice, callous treatment, hurt and pain
That you endured so bravely throughout your short life
'Midst bitter religious and political strife.
By your kith and kin you were pawned, betrayed,
For their naked ambition with your life you paid,
You were a paragon of virtue and innocence, yearning
Only for human comfort and the advancement of your learning,
Author[8] and artists are rekindling your light,
Your courage and fortitude, in the face of your plight.
You are not forgotten — and we are sorry.

---

[8] Historian Alison Weir, author of 'Innocent Traitor' (2006), a novel based on the life of Lady Jane Grey.

# BRUCKNER'S MASS IN E MINOR

It's Bruckner's Mass in E Minor,
Committee says there's nowt finer
To pack the hall from wall to wall,
Than Bruckner's Mass in E Minor.

From Blaina to China,
There's nothing diviner,
They'll have a ball will one and all,
With Bruckner's Mass in E Minor.

Well; call me a whiner,
A whinger and mimer,
But the Dead March in Saul has bugger all
On Bruckner's Mass in E Minor.

# BEDSOCKS AND BROOMSTICKS

Enid and Kirsty are now at the show "Bedsocks and Broomsticks"
No, it's not that, it's more like Bedknobs and Toothpicks.
No, hang on, is it Dreadlocks and Doom flicks?
Or maybe Bed chicks and Moon-rocks?
It's on the tip of my tongue – Broon bread and Slick Jocks,
What the heck is it? Hock bloom and Bread floats…
Wait, I've got it, Dreamboats and Petticoats.

## EDDIE THOMPSON

# WELL THERE WE ARE THEN – IT'S OFFICIAL

Well there we are, that's it then, it's official,
I'm an old man.
I had hoped to delay the onset until I'd reached my three score and ten next year, but no.

Just yesterday, as I entered the city centre shopping mall from the market,
A young man aggressively pulled open a pair of swing doors,
Unaware that I was behind him.
The left-hand door missed me by inches.

His partner, behind me, shouted angrily at him,
"Stephen! There's an old man behind you."

I know she was genuinely concerned about my safety
But I would rather the door had hit me than to have heard those words.

Ageing yes, but old?

Bugger.                                                           December '05

# A WINDSOCK, ANYONE?

I once possessed a condom so big you wouldn't believe,
Please, I beg, don't doubt me, it gains me nowt to deceive
It had cost me thirty shillings, which I thought was a pretty good deal,
It was, after all, reuseable, so at thirty bob, a steal.
It came in a box marked 'Medium' when I'd ordered 'Large' (of course),
It was its length, its enormous length, it might have fitted a horse
It looked like a length of inner-tube, or a sheath from the Middle Ages,
To use it you'd need to be brave, because of its crudeness, courageous
So I returned it to its box, and to the back of a drawer it was hurled,
Scrapping the stupid idea of stuffing the end with the *News of the World*,
Some years later I read that as no one was asking for 'Small',
The product was discontinued, plus the company was going to the wall,
Sizes 'Medium' and 'Large' were relabelled, after a word from the wise,
To flatter inflated male egos, as 'Jumbo' and 'Super-Jumbo' size.

# ONE FOR THE COMMITTEE

So you want a concert that brings the audience to their feet?
Well, I have a cunning plan, which I think is pretty neat
There's the six-nation rugby tournament, what do you think
to singing the national anthem of each? Quick as a blink
as each anthem is sung, each nation would rise to its feet,
Of course they will want to sing along and get behind the beat,
But they're up and out of their seats, bursting with national pride,
Each trying to sing better that those from the other side.
They're not all up together, but when up they're with the choir,
Glad they came to the concert, with their bellies filled with fire.
What d'yer think?

# HYPERBOLE

Hyperbole, it's a word I have no wish to stroke,
In me, a dislike it will always provoke
Was it created by a committee?
Quite possibly, more's the pity,
The second syllable takes the stress,
The others are quieter, that's my guess
Thankfully, it's rarely heard and seldom seen,
But what on earth does it actually mean?
It's a statement that exaggerates a fact,
Used as a figure of speech, attention to attract,
Well, we all do that, but I still dislike the word,
I suppose it has its place, but it looks and sounds absurd.

# LIZ, DEMI-JOHNS AND LSDS

Our good friend Liz once worked in a chemist shop locally,
Where a colleague, being helpful, thoroughly, totally,
Advised, "If a customer requests, you know what, wink wink,
Don't even blink,
Go straight to this drawer marked 'Labour Saving Devices',
Show him the box, let him choose and here's the list of prices."

A man walked in and asked, "Do you happen to have any demi-johns?"
Liz, confused, thought he meant the nudge nudge, wink wink ones,
And pulled out the drawer.
What followed embarrassed her to her core.
"I don't know what you're looking for dear,"
He said, with a grin from ear to ear,
"But if you find a demi-john there, that would be a surprise,
Unless that's a new-fangled name for the super-jumbo size."

# THE TRUNK

There's a trunk in our attic, big, brown and dusty,
With a barrel lid and three locks, all rusty
And big leather handles on either side,
A bottom drawer for a long-ago bride

At the very least it's a hundred years old,
It bears stencilled letters, big, black and bold,
MPJ for Mabel Parry Jones, my long-departed mother,
May God rest her soul, and her troubles smother.

Once lovingly packed with all that she had,
It now sits redundant, empty and sad
What pleasure, what pain, accompanied its filling?
How many porters did she tip with a shilling?

It's lined with a newspaper, brittle and brown,
That once lay under her summer gown
What journeys they took, what stories to tell,
What tragic misfortunes the pair befell

It needs to see sunlight and feel some fresh air,
It needs a new life, a new purpose to share,
I'll do it this summer, so help me I will,
To keep MPJ in my memory still.

## MARK NIEL

I honestly feel
That the poet Mark Niel
Is on the threshold of fame,
It's N-i-e-l,
Mark it well,
There'll be reason to remember the name.

He'll be standing tall,
Known to all,
Except the complete ignoramus
And here in MK
We can honestly say
That we knew him before he was famous.

## PLACE (2)

If place is so important to me, which do I see as mine?
To discover this location, we must factor in a time
So, this is the question, do I have an emotional base?
And the answer currently is, I'm not too sure of my place.

So where and when seem the least distressful?
Where and when seem the most successful?
What places and events dominate my reverie
When giving free rein to an ageing memory?

It's the slopes of Lhergy Frissel,[9] where all was fun and play
Before my adolescence, when the sun shone every day,
As that's where my memory takes me, that must be my place,
So that's the question answered, that's my sort of sacred space.

---

[9] Lhergy Frissel, a wooded hill topped by the Albert Tower, just south of Ramsey on the Isle of Man.

# INNER-CITY FARMING

The temperature's controlled,
Not too hot, not too cold
With just the right amount of light,
Not too dim, not too bright.
The water's measured by the cup,
And see, the seeds are sprouting up.

It's a cellar, yes, but please keep calm,
It's an inner-city cannabis farm
The farmer seeks to buy his yacht,
By tending lots of pots of pot
It's off the menu for you and me,
But others consume it as High Tea.

His wife takes some to sometimes bake
What she calls a Sunshine Cake,
And recently I've heard it said,
That it's now to be found in some granary bread.
With so many such farms here I've often felt,
That we're in the heart of the Cannabis Belt.

# OUR SOULS

He asked me, where do you stand,
On the transmigration of souls?
I told him straight, it should be banned,
With one exception, the Poles.

No no no, you don't understand,
OUR SOULS! OUR SOULS! He shouted,
I tightened the grip on the spade in me hand,
And his sanity I seriously doubted.

He put the question another way,
Are our souls recycled when dead?
I suppose it's possible, I heard myself say,
But it's a transplant I'd seriously dread.

# RECRUITING FOR THE CHORALE

"Make your singing social, join a group, barber – shop, gospel, madrigal, expand your experience into a choral society, operatic society, Gilbert and Sullivan society or rugby club.

Make it communal, it's easier to be carried away in a group. It's controlled mind, disciplined, it's not the primeval roar in gay abandon; although I don't know, at times it could be.

We're not talking Earl Grey tea here. Some thirty years ago I realised that choral singing was becoming something more than just a habit with me and I underwent a two-year spell of singing Perry Como hits, solo, in the sun and sand of the Middle East.

It was agony, and had I not heard and joined the Ahmadi Choral Society singing Christmas Carols in the Kuwaiti desert, I would have been just so much mayonnaise.

Of course there are headaches to be had with some of the stuff; much of it is an acquired taste. Look, keep this under your song sheet, if the government get wise to it they'll slap a tax on it – you know what I'm saying?

I've got to go, Tuesday night is rehearsal night and tonight we're getting blitzed on Berlioz. Think about it."

# BODY PARTS AS METAPHORS

Hair raising/splitting
Brow beating
Brain washing/storming
Ear wigging
Ears burning
Eye catching
Mouth watering
Tongue lashing/twisting
Breathtaking
Voice grating
Mind boggling
Soul searching
Nerve wracking
Lip curling
Chin wagging
Jaw dropping
Neck risking
Spine chilling

Rib tickling
Back stabbing
Heart breaking
Heart warming
Blood curdling
Spleen venting
Waist watching
Navel gazing
Hand wringing
Finger pointing
Stomach churning
Knee jerking
Leg pulling
Buttocks clenching
Arse licking
Toe tapping.

# THE FESTIVE SEASON

Sing mickle melody and look for the mistletoe,
If your luck is in, you'll get a snog afore ye go.

Peace on earth, good will toward men, as it is in heaven,
And here's your Christmas present honey, an AK forty-seven.

To save us from our foolish ways was our Saviour's mission,
Then Praise the Lord, Oh Praise the Lord, and pass the ammunition.

Materialism, commercialism, the cult of the individual,
As if that isn't bad enough, my urine is residual.

A Merry Christmas to both our readers.

## VOICE PROCEDURE

By no means do I regret
Those years spent on a radio net
For they taught me to be brief
Of air-time, a virtual thief
To say your piece, no more, no less,
Be calm, be clear, belie the stress.

Could this be the reason my verses are so short?
Don't waffle, get to the point, that's what I've been taught,
Say what you have to say, and then get off the air,
Others are waiting to send, they'll be pulling out their hair
Already I'm hogging the air-waves, "Get off", I hear you shout,
So, "Message ends" now, reservoir, roger and out.


## GIVE ME AN L

We all dabble in alliteration,
Especially employing the amiable L
We love its lazy proliferation.

What letter relaxes and enhances our leisure?
A vowel? Not likely, it takes the L
To liven, inflate and polish our pleasure.

Admittedly vowels are fairly essential,
But unless they nestle the stalwart L,
They rarely reach their full potential.

It flirts with all who listen, well, almost,
And leaves a flavour on the lips, does L,
Like liquorice, or marmalade on toast.

It lubricates the telling of tales,
And eloquent dialogue demands an L,
So, alert to its values, it's doubled in Wales.

In my mental landscape it has a place,
I can't contemplate a life without L
In my frontal lobes there'd be a blank space,
Without it my life would truly be hell.

    May '06 (A failed Villanelle)

# DEAR TOM

*Risoluto* Dear Tom
*Vigoroso* In trying to follow your instructions
*Deciso* I wrestle daily with the irregular division of time values,
*Mosso* The inversion of triads and second inversion chords,
*Lugubre* The circle of fifths, which makes me dizzy,
*Lamentoso* likewise the tie in arpeggiation.
*Sopirando* But I'm trying, I really am;
*Mesto* even so, I fear that my re-audition will not go well,
*Morendo* Yours, in the fog of a bass clef.
*Placido* Eddie.

    Oct '11

## POST-AUDITION BLUES

It's time to hang up my hymn sheets
As this music 'stuff' my mind unseats
Accidentals, semitones and crotchets,
Time signatures, semibreves and wotsits,
The countless instructions in a foreign tongue
Telling me how the piece should be sung,
When all I wanted to do was to sing,
To take a deep breath and give my voice wing.
So musically illiterate I will have to remain,
And sing in the bath, the pub and the rain.            June '11

# LONGER ONES

Yes, Longer Ones, and I hear you sigh,
And I have no need to wonder why,
For Longer Ones can be a bore,
But then again, there are only four.

# LONGER ONES

## CONTENTS

Time

Travelling Companions

Our Haven

Cambrian Society's Barbecue, Kuwait 1979

# TIME

Time dictates our lives; it gives us order and structure. Learned ones will debate what time actually is, or is not, but here, on ground level, the word is used time and time again to describe events and the gap between events, thus saving a great deal of verbiage. The following examples spring to mind, you can add more.

Times that govern the daily routine:
> Breakfast time, boss's time, dinner/lunch time, boss's time, tea/dinner time, own time, supper time, bed time.

Boss's Time:
> Full time, part time, short time, time and motion study, time sheet, time and a half on Saturdays, double time on Sundays, travelling time, over time, time off, time is money.

Own Time:
> Time for the news, time to put the kettle on, killing time, wasting time, time table, pastime, time for a quick one, "Time Gentlemen Please", ETD, ETA, having the time of one's life.

Times governing sport:
> Half time, time out, full time, extra time, playing for time, record time, time keeper.

Military Times:
> Alpha time, Zulu time, marking time, slow time, quick time, double time, time fuse, time bomb.

Musical Time:
> Time signature, e.g. three-four time, keeping time.

Past, Present and Future Time:
> "Once upon a time…", time immemorial, time honoured, old time, real time, no time like the present, borrowed time, time warp, high time, time enough, father time, time will tell, time machine.

Seasonal/Clock Time:
> Spring time, harvest time, Greenwich Mean Time, Double Summer Time, time zone, time lag, time piece, time keeping.

Punishment Time:
> Doing time, time server, time off for good behaviour, time expired.

Philosophical Time:
> "Time and Tide…".

Time to say Good Bye:
> Time's up, time limit, closing time, The End Time.

# TRAVELLING COMPANIONS

Henrietta the house fly's favourite yarn
Is the time she was swallowed by a young schoolmarm.
It happened last – oh it matters not,
Suffice to say it was extremely hot.

Hetty was flying in a dangerous daze,
She always did, it was one of her ways.
Mathematics she thought, good grief, what a bore,
Too much for Hetty, she looked for the door.

Now low altitude flying for an idle fly
Is fraught with disasters, from which many die.
"She paid the price," I can hear you gloat,
When she disappeared down a yawning throat.

With wings in reverse she tried not to fall,
But down she was washed, not touching the wall.
"At last, the bottom", she said with a moan,
And surprise, surprise, she was not alone.

"Hello", said a voice," I hope you're all right,
"You'll like it down here when you're over the fright.
My name is Fiona", the voice gently said,
"What's yours?" she enquired, and "Have you yet fed?"

What Hetty saw made her squirm,
The polite tender voice belonged to a worm.
"I wonder, I think – I could be right,
I know what you are, a parasite!"

## EDDIE THOMPSON

"Hush my dear, not so loud
You'll hurt my parents, they're frightfully proud.
'Travelling companions' they prefer to be called,
At 'parasites' they'd be most appalled."

"But dear me aren't I rude,
What's your name, and have some food."
Hetty was directed to a piece of fish,
"It must be Friday, her regular dish."

"For fifteen years, much longer than most,
My family's travelled with our lovely host.
It's not always been easy," Fiona then said,
"Two years ago we lost Uncle Fred

Who, with cousin Joe, after much toil,
Was flushed away with castor oil.
An underground future was not Hetty's choice,
She expressed this view with an anxious voice.

"Which way is out, and when can I go?"
"At six tonight, there's a regular flow."
"Good luck," said Fiona, a glint in her eye,
"It would have been nice to travel with a fly."

"Not likely," called Hetty, as she waved cheerio,
"And as from now on, I shall watch where I go."

> For an essay in an English Language "O" level course on
> "Travelling Companions", Bovington, Dorset 1973.

## OUR HAVEN

The location of our haven is close by Linford Wood,
Not an address to grab you, no reason why it should.

It's nothing grand you understand, "Four bed. detached, with garage."
But we've lived in it now for over half our forty years of marriage.

We bought it new in 1980, so it's old for Milton Keynes,
Enid and I, with Kirsty and Gill, in and approaching their teens.

It is for us our haven, our harbour and home port,
Our shelter and protection, our refuge and our fort.

## EDDIE THOMPSON

Fate has yet to reveal why she brought us here,
But she will one day, I'm sure, make it absolutely clear.

It has silently witnessed our smiles and our frowns,
And its walls have recorded our ups and our downs.

Our fledglings have now flown to make homes of their own
And the house may be bored with just Darby and Joan.

It's been home to Crosse and Blackwell, in their three-storey hutch
And Tramp, our singing dog, who gave us all so much.

Yes, we're inner city, yet woodpeckers call each day,
And parked under the plum tree, I've twice seen a jay.

We are well aware, and it's more than just a notion,
That we should return our haven's devotion.

We do when we can, like installing double glazing,
Which deepens our relationship, really it's amazing.

I'm recording this on paper; my feelings say I should,
For our haven and our harbour, close by Linford Wood.  May '05

# CAMBRIAN SOCIETY'S BARBECUE, KUWAIT 1979

Dylan's *Charabanc Outing* was read by Gareth Pugh,
"Heard it before", Iesu yes, but the setting's entirely new.
Cymru Kuwait had assembled, Sian, Gwilym and Enid too,
To gorge themselves with culture and more of Les' brew.


The sun, long gone, had left its card; it was ninety in the dark,
That day the sun had melted Max's tape of Strady Park.
But our hiraeth and nostalgia needed no kindling spark,
As we sang in Les' garden *The Rising of the Lark*.


Accents rang like Port Talbot steel when someone caught my eye,
A Sunday-suited stranger, complete with collar and tie,
A sweating beacon, chapel deacon, to lead us all in song, said I.
From Brum he'd come "Welsh water weaned, enough to join?" There's fly.


How the ladies, the cariads, did shine, like Rhondda diamonds, perhaps,
But rargian, their grannies would roast them for neck lines revealing knee-caps,
Where to look was a problem, my eyes were lured to the traps,
But I don't think Enid noticed my crafty little lapse.


Gwilym told old stories, for the twenty-seventh time,
Big Jim was prompting from the side; he knew them line by line.
And the trees in Les' garden, giants for this clime,
Recalled the woods of Gwydir and its miles of forest pine.


Damp singers in dark corners, mushroomed into song,
We had a bash at Calon Lan and got the words all wrong.
Morgan and Bethania weren't airborne very long,
As the sweat was shed like water, with sugar content strong.

## EDDIE THOMPSON

Wrapped around the eucalyptus, curly tail and all,
Was a fiery bright red dragon, flown over from Porthcawl.
"Iechyd da bob Cymro." I let fly a might bawl,
Then crashed into a flower bed, Duw, I did feel small.

No more hiraeth for us mind, we're going home to stay,
We've had the world and its crazy ways and only yesterday
We packed our bags for Penmachno, (we'll be home to help with the hay)
Where the heat is the warmth of friendship, we're going home – to stay!

February 1979

www.ingramcontent.com/pod-product-compliance
Lightning Source LLC
Chambersburg PA
CBHW061332040426
42444CB00011B/2889